Marc Roche. Macson B

BUSINESS COMMUNICATION IN PLAIN ENGLISH:

How to Use Grammar, Punctuation & Style to Write Effectively in Business and Professional Settings

Business English Originals ©

Marc Roche

&

IDM Business English

www.macsonbell.com

Macson Bell Coaching ®

Copyright © 2022 **Marc Roche**

Marc Roche. Macson Bell ® www.macsonbell.com

Copyright 2022 Marc Roche

www.macsonbell.com

Macson Bell Coaching ®

Copyright © 2022 by Marc Roche & Macson Bell Business & Law. All Rights Reserved.

No part of this business writing, grammar, punctuation and style book may be reproduced, distributed, or transmitted in any form or by any means, including photocopying, recording, or other electronic or mechanical methods, or by any information storage and retrieval system without the prior written permission of the publisher, except in the case of very brief quotations embodied in critical reviews and certain other non-commercial uses permitted by copyright law.

2022 Macson Bell Business English ® Books. All rights reserved

Marc Roche

The information contained in this book is intended for informational purposes only and should not be construed as legal advice on any subject matter. You should not act or refrain from acting based on any content included in this book without seeking legal or other professional advice.

"Good communication is just as stimulating as black coffee, and it's just as hard to sleep after."-

Anne Morrow Lindbergh

Business Grammar, Style, and Punctuation in Use 9
Dedication 10
Books in This Series 13
Contributors & Influencers 16
Get Marc Roche's Entire Template Library FOR FREE 18
Why This Book? 19
Chapter 1. Initial Housekeeping 22
   How to Organise 23
   How to Declutter 25
   How to Influence 28
Chapter 2. How to Write Strong Sentences 37
   Expressing the Active 38
   Fixing Weak Statements 40
Chapter 3. How to Be Diplomatic in Writing 43
   Diplomacy 44
   Innefficiencies 46
   Converting from Passive to Active Voice 50
Chapter 4. Common Problems 54
   Consistency in the Use of Terminology 55
   Overly Elaborate Language 56
   Paragraphs 60
   "Who" vs. "Whom" 61
   Standard Words & Phrases 62
   How to Summarize Information 64
Chapter 5. Business Style & Punctuation 66
   The Comma 67
   Commenting Clauses VS Defining Clauses 68
   Semicolons 71
   Possessives & Apostrophes 73
   Lists 75
   Adding Information with Parenthetical Expressions 77
   Days and Dates 79

Non-restrictive Relative Clauses 80
Dependent Clauses 82
Independent Clauses 85
Participial Phrases 87
Loose Sentences 89
Similar Meaning & Function = Similar Form 91
Parentheses 95
Quotations 96
Providing References 99
Word Order 101
Split Infinitives 111
Subject-Verb Agreement 118
Verbs VS Nouns 128
Ending with a Preposition 131
"That" & "Which" 134
Conjunctions 136
The Rule of the Last Antecedent 141
Adding Descriptive Information with -ing phrases 144

Thank you 147

What Next? 149

700+ Business Communication Resources FOR FREE 150

Free Bonus: 300+ Presentation Templates for PowerPoint 151

About the Author 152

"Grammar is not a set of arbitrary rules; it is a compact between people who wish to understand each other."

Robert Breault

Business Grammar, Style, and Punctuation in Use

Business Communication in Plain English, provides a highly-structured framework under which professionals and business students can significantly improve their knowledge of English grammar, style, and punctuation to become more confident and effective writers.

You will be taken through the language structures that tend to create the most problems in the real world and encouraged to review them through highly focused exercises, which target grammar, competence and confidence in international business communication.

Dedication

This book is dedicated to one of the brightest, bravest, and most inspirational people in my life. My aunty Carmel is not just my aunty, she got me started in this crazy journey of teaching and writing. I don't know where I would be without her help, guidance, and inspiration during and immediately after my teacher training.

Lots of love,

Marc

Who is this book for?

This book aims to help two types of readers:

1) Readers whose first language is not English
2) Native English speakers looking to brush up on their grammar, punctuation, and style to become more confident, professional and persuasive writers.

This book aims to help professionals with:

- Business Writing
- Essential Business Grammar
- Punctuation in formal and professional settings
- Business Writing Style
- The Commonly Confused Language Structures that Cause the Most Problems in Real-World Scenarios
- Report Writing
- Proposal Writing
- Data Presentation
- Persuasive Writing in Business and Professional Contexts
- Communication in English

This is Not a Vocabulary Book

We are not focusing on specialized business concepts here, but instead, we are concentrating on **language structures that you can use to be clearer and more persuasive.** We will also look at the grammar that often causes the most issues in real-world situations.

In the next few chapters, you will practice and perfect the basic building blocks of clear, professional communication in English to present yourself in the best possible light to clients, colleagues, and other stakeholders.

If you follow the advice and the exercises in this book, you will write clear, concise, and well-polished sentences to gain credibility and avoid miscommunication and conflict from the start.

Marc Roche. Macson Bell ® www.macsonbell.com

Books in This Series

Amazon Associate Links

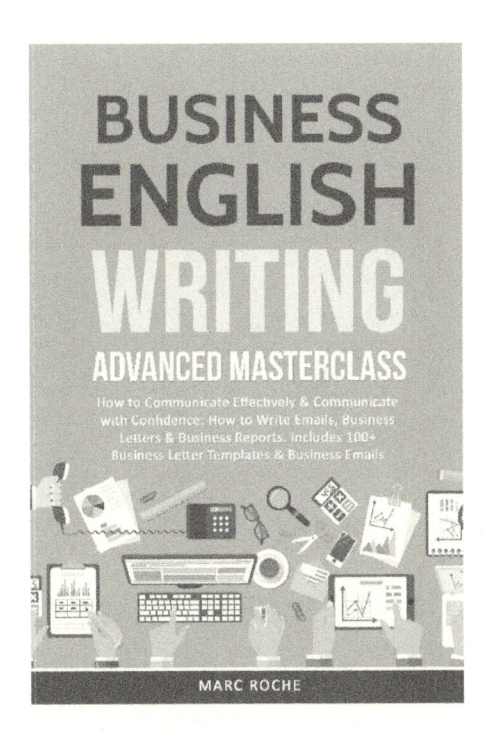

Business English Writing:

Advanced Masterclass by Marc Roche

Business Email: Write to Win by Marc Roche

Marc Roche. Macson Bell ® www.macsonbell.com

Email Writing: Advanced by Marc Roche

Contributors & Influencers

If you are interested in business writing and communication, I can recommend a few other books that will complement this one.

Some of these books are mine and others have been written by people far smarter and more accomplished than me.

The following authors have written fantastic books on the subject, and they deserve mention. These are my Business communication rock stars, and without their contribution through their work, I would never have been able to write this book.

If you have never read their books, buy them and read them over and over again. It's that simple.

Marc Roche. Macson Bell ® www.macsonbell.com

Books by Other Authors: Amazon Associate Links

On Writing Well: The Classic Guide to Writing Nonfiction by William Zinsser

HBR Guide to Better Business Writing by Bryan A. Garner

Writing that Works by Kenneth Roman

Business Writing Today: A Practical Guide by Natalie Cavanor

Business and Professional Writing A Basic Guide by Paul MacRae

Everyday Business Storytelling by Janine Kurnoff

Get Marc Roche's Entire Template Library FOR FREE

Sign up for the no-spam newsletter and get an introductory book and more exclusive content, all for free.

Details can be found at the end of the book.

Why This Book?

Learn the Rules Now, Break Them Later

Welcome. I'm Marc Roche; I'm an author, coach, and founder of Macson Bell Coaching® www.macsonbell.com.

In this book, I will show you how to transform your ability to persuade and influence with clear, simple grammar. No complications or pretences, just clean communication.

Anyone who has had to battle an onslaught of objections, misunderstandings, and questions will understand how career-changing it can be to master the craft and science of writing.

As legendary American executive Lee Iacocca put it, *"you can have brilliant ideas, but if you can't get them across, your ideas won't get you anywhere."*

This book, and the next book in this series, are about subtly persuading through the understanding of psychology, language, and grammar.

As an educated professional, it's very likely that a large part of your day-to-day work centers around writing. But a client or partner who receives a poorly written email may hesitate to send further work your way.

Business Communication in Plain English: How to Use Grammar, Punctuation & Style to Write Effectively in Business & Professional Settings will transform your communication skills with simple lessons and enjoyable activities to boost your writing, confidence, and performance.

Building advanced level business writing requires more than gimmicks and set phrases. This book is straightforward, with simple lessons, to help transform you into a clear and confident communicator.

It's Not All About Grammar

This business writing guidebook should not be read as a complete presentation of the 'rules' of English.

With this Business Writing book, you can expect to:

- Improve your business writing and speaking.
- Feel more confident, particularly when you have to write to colleagues, clients, suppliers, and other stakeholders.
- Boost your performance and general efficiency at work through better writing.
- Lower your general stress levels by communicating clearly and correctly.

Chapter 1. Initial Housekeeping

How to Organise

Generally speaking, information in sentences should go from:

old to new

familiar to unfamiliar

simple to complex

Although this ensures a logical flow of ideas, don't take it as a strict rule. You can break this organisation 'rule' whenever you want, if it makes your writing more appealing without confusing the reader. Your priority should always be to communicate clearly while keeping your reader engaged. **Remember that a perfectly clear and polished sentence is useless if nobody pays attention to it.**

End sentences with:
- Information that needs build-up and is highly relevant to your argument.
- Any ideas that you will expand upon in the next few sentences.

- New concepts, or issues that the reader may not recognise.

Sentence length:

Use short sentences with one main point to highlight information. Short sentences carry a lot more weight, so use them to transmit your most important conclusions and arguments. You can also use shorter sentences when changing topics. This adds emphasis to the change and leads the reader from one mental image to another.

How to Declutter

Reading and listening are all about interpretation. How we interpret a message is influenced by many things, but the focus of the message is one of the most important factors. We see this trick used every day in news headlines, bulletins, business reports, and even scientific papers. How the writer or speaker presents the ideas influences how we interpret the situation and the events.

When writing formally, many people's initial instinct is to clutter the beginning of a sentence with overly complicated yet unimportant language. When we do this, our reader loses concentration.

If you're trying to persuade, you need your reader's attention, so keep sentences as simple as possible and aim to make a good impression from the start.

The human brain has developed to be as efficient as possible at gathering large amounts of information from its environment. It has evolved to evaluate things based on the most readily-available information and then dive deeper if needed. This is an automatic process and it happens all the time. It's the reason why you can't seem to get into that new series, and the reason why you bought that new novel. Your brain assessed the reputation, blurb, and cover. We judge everything by its cover at the start. Whether we like to admit it or not, appearances matter.

Because our brains are constantly scanning for important information they automatically focus more on the beginning of sentences and paragraphs. This is why when you read a sentence that starts with irrelevant information; your mind often switches off.

Example:

According to a nationwide study carried out in 2019 by the National Institute of Statistics, 100,000 minors don't have access to adequate schooling.

This is OK, but if we want to focus the reader's attention on the fact that 100,000 minors don't have access to adequate schooling, it might be better if we write:

100,000 minors don't have access to adequate schooling, according to a nationwide study carried out in 2019 by the National Institute of Statistics.

How to Influence

Let's look at the same examples from above.

Example:

According to a nationwide study carried out in 2019 by the National Institute of Statistics, 100,000 minors don't have access to adequate schooling.

As mentioned above, this is OK, but it would normally be better to focus the start of the sentence on the most important information, which is that 100,000 minors don't have access to adequate schooling UNLESS you aimed to draw attention away from this fact.

Compare them again:

According to a nationwide study carried out in 2019 by the National Institute of Statistics, 100,000 minors don't have access to adequate schooling.

VS.

100,000 minors don't have access to adequate schooling, according to a nationwide study carried out in 2019 by the National Institute of Statistics.

The first sentence takes some attention and, therefore, importance away from the fact that 100,000 minors don't have *adequate schooling*.

On the other hand, the second sentence makes it the prime focus. *100,000 minors don't have access to adequate schooling*. The secondary information about the study and when it was carried out takes a back seat and is therefore perceived, on a subconscious level, as less relevant by the reader.

This simple trick is powerful, and it is something skilled writers and speakers knowingly implement all the time.

Before writing, get used to thinking about your objective.

What do you want the reader to focus on?

Put your most attractive words and concepts first or last, depending on your answer to this question.

Exercise One

Form sentences using the words provided. Write two versions for each sentence to switch the focus of the message, as shown in the example below. You can omit or add words if you think it will improve the sentence. Remember to focus on the message.

Example:

This/ material/mainly/ is/ used /car/ steering/ wheels/ of/ its/ durability /and/ light weight/ making/ because/ for

This material is mainly used for making car steering wheels because of its durability and light weight.

VS.

Because of its durability and light weight, this material is mainly used for making car steering wheels.

1. having/ this/ quarter/ are/ down/ last/ year/, despite/ the/ company/ had/ an/ increased/ and/ fewer/ overheads/ profits/ for/ workload/40%/ on/

_____

VS.

_____

2. 'Opening Doors to Women in Technology Award'/to /inform /you/ / earlier/ this week/ Claire Curtis/ joined/ our/ team/ in/ 2018/ as/

a/ technology/ consultant/ received/ the/ news/ that/ she/ has/ I/ am/ delighted/ been/shortlisted /for/ the

---

vs.

Exercise Two

Transform each sentence to shift the focus of the message. You can change the order and the words used.

Example:

Initial investment is vital to the success of this project.

VS

The success of this project depends upon initial investment.

1. Popular and cost-effective, this service should be added to our regular client package.

2. Key products are missing from this month's inventory

3. *The entire meeting was dedicated to discussing new business.*

You can check your answers to exercises 1 and 2 on the next page.

Answers

Exercise One:

having/ this/ quarter/ are/ down/ last/ year/, despite/ the/ company/ had/ an/ increased/ and/ fewer/ overheads/ profits/ for/ workload/40%/ on/

Profits for this quarter are down 40% on last year, despite the company having had an increased workload and fewer overheads.

VS.

Despite the company having had an increased workload and fewer overheads, profits for this quarter are down 40% on last year.

'Opening Doors to Women in Technology Award'/to /inform /you/ / earlier/ this week/ Claire Curtis/ joined/ our/ team/ in/ 2018/ as/ a/ technology/ consultant/ received/ the/ news/ that/ she/ has/ I/ am/ delighted/ been/shortlisted /for/ the

I am delighted to inform you that, earlier this week, Claire Curtis, who joined our team in 2018 as a technology consultant, received the news that she has been shortlisted for the 'Opening Doors to Women in Technology Award.'

VS

Claire Curtis has been shortlisted for the 'Opening Doors to Women in Technology Award,' I am delighted to inform you. Claire joined our team in 2018 as a technology consultant.

Exercise Two:

Popular and cost-effective, this service should be added to our regular client package.

VS.

This service should be added to our regular client package, as it is popular and cost-effective.

Key products are missing from this month's inventory

VS.

This month's inventory is missing key products.

The entire meeting was dedicated to discussing new business.

VS.

Discussing new business was the focus of the entire meeting.

Chapter 2. How to Write Strong Sentences

Expressing the Active

It's a good idea to use the active voice if possible, as it makes for more organized, clear, and vivid sentences in general. Passive voice sentences are often longer and use more obscure word combinations, but they're also less specific and can lead to disconnected readers.

Examples:

Simple Present

Active: *Meadow Soprano handles the new accounts.*

Passive: *The new accounts are handled (by Meadow Soprano).*

Present Continuous

Active: *Meadow Soprano is handling the new accounts.*

Passive: *The new accounts are being handled (by Meadow Soprano).*

Simple Past

Active: *Meadow Soprano handled the new accounts.*

Passive: *The new accounts were handled (by Meadow Soprano).*

Present Perfect

Active: *Meadow Soprano has handled the new accounts.*

Passive: *The new accounts have been handled (by Meadow Soprano).*

Past Perfect

Active: *Meadow Soprano had handled the new accounts.*

Passive: *The new accounts had been handled (by Meadow Soprano).*

Future

Active: *Meadow Soprano will handle the new accounts.*

Passive: *The new accounts will be handled (by Meadow Soprano).*

Auxiliary Verb "Must"

Active: *Meadow Soprano must handle the new accounts.*

Passive: *The new accounts must be handled (by Meadow Soprano).*

Fixing Weak Statements

The active voice usually is more straightforward and more powerful than the passive:

Most of our New York office will be attending the conference.

This is clearer and more concise than:

The conference will be attended by most of our New York office.

Using the passive when it's not needed can sometimes produce ridiculous sentences like:

The conference will be attended by me next week.

If you try to fix it by removing "*by me,*" you turn it into an indefinite:

The conference will be attended next week.

The sentence is now too unclear.

Who is going to be attending the conference?

Is it an unknown group of people?

Are we referring to people in general?

It's always better to write and say: *I will be attending the conference next week.*

Summary:
- Use the active voice most of the time.
- The active voice carries more power, particularly in writing.

Many weak statements can be made lively and emphatic by using a verb in the active voice and avoiding fillers like *'the reason why'* **or** *'the reason that...'.*

Example 1:

The reason why she resigned from her last role was that her health became impaired.

It would be much better to express the above sentence as:

Failing health compelled her to resign from her last role.

Example 2:

It wasn't too long before I felt regret for how I'd behaved.

It would be much better to express the above sentence as:

I soon regretted my behavior.

Chapter 3. How to Be Diplomatic in Writing

Diplomacy

The passive voice gets a terrible reputation among writers, partly because so many people overuse it to portray a 'professional tone,' and end up using it incorrectly. However, this doesn't mean that you should completely discard it, as it's often convenient and necessary in business writing.

Contrary to what many writing books would have you believe, the passive voice is vital when you need to draw focus away from the person performing the action. Maybe the person or thing that performs the action isn't significant, or it could even be a sensitive or delicate matter. Using the passive voice is especially useful for texts where you need to come across as objective, such as legal texts or company policies and regulations.

As Mr. Friedrich Nietzsche once said, *"we often refuse to accept an idea merely because the tone in which it has been expressed is unsympathetic to us."*

Take the following example:

You must not leave the door open at any time.

This sentence is clear and direct, but it also sounds confrontational and condescending.

The door must not be left open at any time is a better option, because it avoids pointing the finger directly at "you".

Similarly:

We will not include accessories

is saying: 'we, the greedy, difficult company who want to sell you this product to make money, are denying you all the accessories that we have just shown you in this product picture so that you have to go and buy them separately and we can make more money off you.'

It's more factual and less confrontational if we simply use the passive voice and write.

Accessories (are) not included.

Innefficiencies

As we saw at the beginning of the chapter, readers are more focused at the beginning of sentences and paragraphs, and quickly lose focus if you fail to grab their attention. Nothing makes the mind wander like a long, pointless start to a sentence.

In the following active voice sentence:

We will donate over $175,000.

The start of the sentence focuses on "we". It tells the reader that we will do something. The most attractive part of the sentence (*Over $175,000*) doesn't appear until the end. This fails to capitalise on an opportunity to hook the reader from the start.

If we change the sentence to:

Over $175,000 will be donated.

we start with the most attractive information, really changing the focus in the reader's mind. It's literally more bang for your buck.

So, passive or active?

It all depends on the message you have and your objective.

Try not to make one passive verb depend directly on another in a sentence.

They have been proven to have been investigated by authorities.

The sentence above would be better if we changed it to:

It has been proven that they were investigated by authorities.

Or

It has been proven that authorities investigated them.

A typical inefficiency in passive sentences is to write a noun that expresses the entire action of the sentence as the subject.

If we do this, we have no choice but to use a redundant verb that adds no meaning to the sentence.

An analysis of the infrastructure was done in 2019.

VS

The infrastructure was analyzed in 2019.

Summary:

Use the Passive

1. To emphasize the action itself instead of the Person or Thing that 'Does' the Action.

"After four days of negotiations, an agreement was reached by the managing partners."

2. To Be Tactful

"The events were misconstrued."

"Mistakes were made."

3. When the doer is unknown or not important

"Every month, hundreds of people are left homeless."

4. To Set a Detached or Official Tone (Signs or Notices)

"Guests are not allowed to smoke."

Converting from Passive to Active Voice

1. Move the doer of the action to the start of the sentence and move the person or thing that receives the action after the verb.

2. Adapt the verb form as needed.

3. If no doer is mentioned in the passive sentence, you can often logically infer who or what acted.

   For example, in the sentence.

   All of Nike's factories were pulled out of China.

   Even though we haven't explicitly said that *Nike* pulled the factories out of China, it is implied in the sentence that since we haven't mentioned the person or group who pulled them out, it must be Nike itself. Therefore, *Nike* is the doer, and the factories are the object that receives the action.

All of Nike's factories were pulled out of China.

⤵

Nike pulled all its factories out of China.

You have to do the exact opposite if you want to change an active sentence into a passive one.

For example:

Do not close the window.

⤵

The window should not be closed.

Or in the positive

The window should be kept open at all times.

Exercise

Decide whether each of the following sentences is active or passive. If you think the sentence doesn't need changing, just write "no change" next to it. If you think changing it from active to passive or vice-versa would improve it, go ahead and rewrite the sentence.

1. Staff don't speak English at the front desk.

....

2. A report was given to him by Mary.

....

3. Many people know Bavaria for its cuisine.

....

4. You should reconsider the new policy you are trying to implement.

....

Answers

1. **Staff don't speak English at the front desk.**

    No change is needed here, usually. This can be expressed as a complaint or a simple observation, depending on the tone of voice.

2. **A report was given to him by Mary.**

    Mary gave him a report.

3. **Many people know Bavaria for its cuisine.**

    Bavaria is known for its cuisine.

4. **You need to change the new policy you are trying to implement.**

    The new policy needs to be changed.
    This is much less personal and confrontational.

Chapter 4.

Common Problems

What follows in this section is a review of some of the most problematic mistakes in formal business writing. These are mistakes that both native and non-native English speakers often make, sometimes without ever realizing.

To err is human, but if we want to give the best possible impression of ourselves in writing, we must keep our mistakes to a bare minimum.

Please note that this is by no means an exhaustive list of possible errors but instead a handpicked selection of some of the most common ones.

Consistency in the Use of Terminology

Firstly, it's important to be consistent when using terminology, particularly when referring to the parties involved. This means being consistent in the names we use to identify things, places, companies, and people.

Suddenly switching the label that we give to something in a document can lead to confusion, frustration, and even miscommunication.

The writer must choose the label they will use and stick to it throughout the document.

For example:

'the organization,' 'the company,' 'XYZ PLC,' 'the defendant,' 'the respondent,' 'the employee,' 'the employer,' etc.

Overly Elaborate Language

Contracts often contain extremely formal language, including words such as:

hereupon, herewith, hereafter, hereto, herein, hereby, hereof, hereunder, hereinbefore, hereinafter; thereafter, thereby, therein, thereinbefore, thereon, thereof, thereupon, thereunder, therewith; wherein, whereof, whereon, etc.

- This type of language is not usually appropriate in business communication.
- The writer should avoid using Latin and French if the word or phrase can be written in plain English.

Exercise

Match the overly elaborate language 1-16, with its more direct, realistic equivalent, under the 'Realistic Equivalents' section.

1. Hereupon:
2. Herewith:
3. Herein:
4. Hereto:
5. Hereunder:
6. Hereof:
7. Hereafter:
8. Heretofore:
9. Herewith:
10. Hereinafter:
11. Hereby:
12. Thereinafter:
13. Thereinbefore:
14. Therein:
15. Thereafter:
16. Aforementioned:

Realistic Equivalents

- after that
- from now on (for time)
- included from now on in this document.
- underneath this line
- previously mentioned.
- inside this document.
- together with this document
- included earlier in a document
- included in a document afterward.
- of this event/fact
- Following immediately after this (at this stage).
- Therefore
- Subsequently (afterward)
- inside that document
- related to this document
- previously (before this moment in time)

Check your answers on the next page.

Answers

1. Hereupon: Subsequently (afterward)
2. Herewith: Following immediately after this (at this stage).
3. Herein: inside this document.
4. Hereto: of this event/fact
5. Hereunder: underneath this line
6. Hereof: related to this document
7. Hereafter: from now on (for time)
8. Heretofore: previously (before this moment in time)
9. Herewith: together with this document
10. Hereinafter: included from now on in this document.
11. Hereby: therefore
12. Thereinafter: included in a document afterward.
13. Thereinbefore: included earlier in a document
14. Therein: inside that document
15. Thereafter: after that
16. Aforementioned: previously mentioned.

Here is a great article with some examples of words that you can eliminate: https://law.utexas.edu/faculty/wschiess/legalwriting/2008/06/ten-legal-words-and-phrases-we-can-do.html

Paragraphs

- Use the first sentence of each paragraph to outline the topic of the paragraph.
- Paragraphs with only one sentence are rarely appropriate.
- Long, complicated paragraphs are difficult and exhausting for readers.
- Separate topics always go in separate paragraphs. Do not fuse separate topics into one paragraph.
- Every paragraph should focus on one topic.
- You can often split long paragraphs into shorter paragraphs. When a topic is too large or complex for one paragraph, it should be split into several paragraphs.

"Who" vs. "Whom"

When a pronoun is the <u>subject</u> of a verb, we need to use "who."

Example: *Mr. Brown overheard Jack and Jill,* ***who*** *were talking about the contract.*

When a pronoun is the <u>object</u> of a verb or preposition, we use "whom."

Example: *Mr. Brown saw the man with* ***whom*** *Jill was talking about the contract.*

This rule has become more of a guideline for formal writing in modern English. It is acceptable to use "who" instead of "whom," but there will be readers who adhere strictly to the original rule and who will notice if we don't follow it exactly. Following this guideline can make our writing stiffer and less communicative. It may also make our sentences needlessly more complicated in some cases, but it will avoid potential issues with more traditional audiences.

Trick: If you can swap the word for *"he"* or *"she,"* use ***"who."*** If you can swap it for *"him"* or *"her,"* use ***"whom."***

Standard Words & Phrases

Standard words and phrases that are often used incorrectly include the words:

'advice' noun VS *'advise'* verb.

'tortuous' VS *'tortious.'*

'counsel' (barrister) VS *'council'* (local authority).

'principle' (fundamental concept, or doctrine) VS *'principal'* (a person who employs an agent, etc.).

'Hone in on' vs. *'Home in on'*

To *'home in on'* is when we direct our attention and focus toward something, or when our attention and focus are drawn to something.

Example:

*The prosecution **homed in on** the defendant's argument.*

One of the main meanings of "hone" is to sharpen or perfect something like a skill.

Example:

*The defendant **honed** her argument after the prosecution **homed in on** her claims that she did not understand the contract she had signed.*

How to Summarize Information

When summarizing, you should preferably use the present tense or the past tense, depending on which is more suitable. If you use the present tense, express past events in the present perfect; if you use the past, in past perfect.

As a result of the circumstances outlined above, this project cannot be delivered by the agreed deadline. My team and I have made every effort to avoid this delay and offer our sincerest apologies for any inconvenience caused.

A past tense in indirect communication must remain in its original tense.

The manufacturers accept that their machinery was at fault.

Apart from the exceptions noted, whichever tense you choose, use throughout. Changing from one tense to another looks disorganized and takes power away from your communication.

In presenting the statements or the thoughts of someone else, as in summarizing a report or a speech, avoid inserting expressions like "s*he stated*," "she *added*," "*the speaker then went on to say*," or any other similar phrase. Instead of wasting words by constantly telling the reader or listener that "s*he stated*," "she *added*," or "*the speaker then went on to say*," inform your audience that you are providing a summary and then focus on communicating the important information.

Chapter 5. Business Style & Punctuation

The Comma

Commas are designed to signal natural breaks or pauses within sentences and lists. However, they can also be placed following an introductory clause.

For example:

"Although the judge stated that she understood the defendant's difficult position, she denied bail due to the flight risk that he posed."

We can also use commas to add extra information in the middle of the sentence. Instead of using brackets, we can add two commas to separate the clause.

For example: *"Mr. Bryan A. Garner's email, which clearly stated the terms of the agreement, was received by Mr. Antonio Soprano on 15th May 2021."*

instead of

"Mr. Bryan A. Garner's email (which clearly stated the terms of the agreement) was received by Mr. Antonio Soprano on 15th May 2021."

Commenting Clauses VS Defining Clauses

'Commenting clauses' add extra information to a sentence while 'defining clauses' literally define whom we are referring to. We use commas to add extra background information with commenting clauses, but we omit the commas when using a defining clause to clarify whom we are talking about.

Example of a commenting clause:

"Mr. J. Pinkman, who was on probation at the time, drove to 308 Negra Arroyo Lane with a briefcase containing 10,000 USD in unmarked bills on the morning of March 6th, 2013."

Example of a defining clause:

"The company that presented the tender informed us that they were no longer in the position to offer us the service."

Here is an example of how this rule can change the meaning of your messages:

"As Mr. Wydick informed us, all set up costs incurred by new small businesses, who do not qualify for financial assistance from the IRS, can be covered using an interest-free loan from Trachtman Bank Ltd."

The commas mean that *'who do not qualify'* is a commenting clause, adding extra background information about *'new small businesses.'* The sentence says that no new small businesses qualify for financial assistance from the IRS.

If we want to communicate that only some small businesses do not qualify for assistance, we need to eliminate commas.

"As Mr. Wydick informed us, all set up costs incurred by new small businesses who do not qualify for financial assistance from the IRS can be covered using an interest-free loan from Trachtman Bank Ltd."

The meaning in this second example is completely different. We have now used a 'defining clause' that specifies the type of new small businesses we are talking about. In this sentence, we are only talking about new small businesses that do not qualify for assistance, not those that do. As you can see, this is extremely important when it comes to writing within legal and business contexts.

Semicolons

We apply a semicolon (;) when we need to unite two closely related independent clauses (without conjunction). We add a comma to join two independent clauses closely related and separated by a conjunction.

Examples:

So, if our core message is:

The contract states that BDL Ltd. must inform XTZ Properties of all proposed building work at least 30 days prior to its approval, it does not specify who is responsible for paying for the administrative fees involved.

We can express it like this:

The contract states that BDL Ltd. must inform XTZ Properties of all proposed building work at least 30 days prior to its approval; **however,** *it does not specify who is responsible for paying for the administrative fees involved.*

While the word "However" is not needed in this particular example, we are using it to emphasize the connection between the two clauses and help our readers understand our message more clearly.

Another option would be to write:

The contract states that BDL Ltd. must inform XTZ Properties of all proposed building work at least 30 days prior to its approval, **but** *it does not specify who is responsible for paying for the administrative fees involved.*

Possessives & Apostrophes

Make the possessive singular of nouns by adding *'s*, whatever the final consonant.

For example:
Charles's colleague
Burns's email
the project's main goal

Exceptions:

You may also encounter nouns that finish with an 's' written like this: 'Charles' colleague' and 'Burns' email. Writing it like this, is also generally acceptable, but if you're not sure, it's best to follow the initial example and simply add 's regardless of what the final consonant is.

Other possible exceptions are the possessives of ancient proper names ending in *-es* and *-is*, the possessive *Jesus'*, and some forms like *for conscience' sake*, *for righteousness' sake*.

Possessives such as:

hers

his

yours

ours

theirs

its

oneself

do not carry apostrophe.

Lists

In a list of three or more things with a single conjunction, use a comma after each term. You can choose to use an Oxford comma* before the last one or not, depending on your preference, but be aware that it could make some sentences unclear.

Example:

- *laptops, phones, and other electronic devices*
- *wine, beer, or spirits*
- *They opened the meeting, discussed the main issues concerning the project, and left before we were able to raise our concerns.*

The Oxford Comma

The Oxford comma is a comma placed before the last item in a series of three or more. Many style guides advise against using it, and many style guides advise writers to use it. For practical reasons, this guide advises in favor of using it, as it can avoid miscommunication in some instances. For example, *I have received confirmation from the engineering team, Thom and Joe.*

This is ambiguous, as we might not know whether the engineering team are Tom and Joe, or whether Thom and Joe are separate entities in the list. It's much clearer; therefore, to write, *I have received confirmation from the engineering team, Tom, and Joe.*

If you're interested in seeing the potential business issues that misusing the Oxford comma can cause, search online for the case of the Oxford comma dispute settled for $5 million!

Adding Information with Parenthetical Expressions

Enclose parenthetical expressions between commas.

The best way to see Berlin, unless you are pressed for time, is to walk around the center.

- If there is very little interruption to the sentence flow, you don't need to add commas.

- What you can't do is add one comma and omit the other.

Examples of wrong use of commas in this case are:

The project founder, Jack Glibb sent me an email yesterday,

Or

Jack Glibb you will be pleased to hear, is coming to New York for the meeting,...

If there is a conjunction before a parenthetic expression, put the first comma before the conjunction, not after it.

He welcomed me into his office, and unaware that I had already spoken about the matter with his manager, (he) proceeded to tell me all about the new project.

Days and Dates

The following are always parenthetic and should be enclosed between commas (or, at the end of the sentence, between comma and period):

- Years that form part of a date.

- Days of the month that appear after the day of the week.

> *June 12, 1999*
> *September to November, 2019.*
> *Wednesday, September 16, 2020.*

Abbreviations like *Jr.* and *etc.* follow the same rule.

Business Names

In the names of businesses, the last comma is usually omitted,

> *Brown, Shipley & Co.*

Non-restrictive Relative Clauses

Relative clauses that don't help us identify the noun that went before them, and other clauses indicating time or location of events.

Example:

The manager, who had initially been quite hostile, became a lot friendlier once we explained our idea.

In this sentence, the clause '*who had initially been quite hostile*' doesn't specify one manager from a group of two or more managers; there's only one manager present in the situation described.

The sentence combines two separate statements to provide complete information. The clause '*who had initially been quite hostile*' gives extra information for a fuller picture of the situation's dynamics. It could even be expressed as two separate sentences, but it wouldn't be as efficient:

The manager had initially been quite hostile. He became friendlier once we'd explained our idea.

With different punctuation, the meaning is different. Compare the various meanings of these two sentences:

The manager, who had initially been quite hostile, became a lot friendlier once we explained our idea.

VS.

The manager who had at first been quite hostile, became friendlier once we explained our idea.

In the second sentence, we're talking about a particular manager from a group of possible managers present during the meeting. We can't divide this sentence into two statements like we could with the first example.

Dependent Clauses

Phrases or dependent clauses that go just before or after the main clause of a sentence.

Partly through smart investments, partly through joint ventures, they have managed to grow their profits by 40% in the last twelve months and have become pioneers with the release of their new software, as well as the opening of a new call-center.

Comma before conjunctions that introduce co-ordinate clauses.

The economic outlook is bleak, but there is still one chance of avoiding disaster.

The above sentence is perfectly acceptable, but it can give the impression of being a little unprofessional sometimes, mainly when we use this style repeatedly. It gives the impression of being improvised and slightly lazy if we just use the same structure over and over.

The sentence could be rewritten as follows:

Although the economic outlook is bleak, there is still one chance of avoiding disaster.

Or we could switch the subordinate clauses for phrases:

In this bleak economic outlook, there is still one chance of avoiding disaster.

Offering Relief

You need to offer your reader some relief at times.

If you make your sentences too uniformly compact and periodic, the style becomes too robotic, formal, and solemn without an occasional loose sentence. It is best to use a combination of all three structures given above.

Dependent clauses, or introductory phrases set off by a comma, which go before the second independent clause, do not need a comma after the conjunction.

Example: *The economic outlook is bleak, but if we are prepared to act promptly, there is still one chance of avoiding disaster.*

Independent Clauses

Independent clauses in a sentence

If you need to write a single sentence with two or more grammatically complete clauses that are not joined by a conjunction, use a semicolon instead of a comma.

James's presentations are entertaining; they are full of valuable information.

It's nearly half-past five; we cannot reach the meeting room before half-past six.

You can also write each of the above examples as two separate sentences:

James's presentations are entertaining. They are full of valuable information.

It's nearly half-past five. We cannot reach the meeting room before half-past six.

Use a comma if you add a conjunction.

James's presentations are entertaining, as they are full of valuable information.

It's nearly half-past five, and we cannot reach the meeting room before half-past six.

Participial Phrases

If you use a participial phrase at the start of a sentence, it must refer to the person or thing that performs the action in that sentence.

Talking to Jenna, I realized that I need a new challenge.

The word *talking* refers to the doer of the sentence (*me* in this case), not to Jenna.

The same rules apply when you start sentences with participial phrases that carry a conjunction, preposition, noun in apposition, adjective, or adjective phrase before them.

On arriving in Chicago, my assistant met me at the station.

VS

When I arrived (or, On my arrival) in Chicago, my assistant met me at the station.

A manager with a proven track record, they have entrusted him with setting up the new department.

VS

A manager with a proven track record, he has been entrusted with setting up the new department.

Loose Sentences

Although a loose sentence now and then can be useful to provide relief for the reader, a series of them soon becomes monotonous and tedious. Therefore, if you aim for a semi-formal or formal tone, try to avoid using too many loose sentences.

People often write whole paragraphs around loose sentences, using: *but, and, so, which,* who, *where, when,* and *while.*

The third presentation of the conference was given this afternoon, and a large audience was in attendance. Mr. Edward Appleton spoke first about his team's findings, and his colleague Ms. Freda Burns presented the supporting evidence. The former showed himself to be very knowledgeable in his field, while the latter proved herself fully deserving of her excellent reputation. The interest aroused by the presentation has been very gratifying to the Committee, and it is planned to hold a similar conference annually hereafter. The fourth presentation will be given on Tuesday, May 4, when an equally fascinating program will be presented.

The paragraph above can be improved by injecting some variety into the sentence structures.

Suppose you find that you have written a series of sentences of the type described. In that case, you can edit enough of them to remove the monotony, replacing them with simple sentences, with sentences of two clauses joined by a semicolon, with periodic sentences of two clauses, periodic or loose sentences, of three clauses-whichever best expresses your ideas.

Similar Meaning & Function = Similar Form

It's best to have a similar form and structure for sentences that carry a similar meaning or function within the paragraph. This helps the reader identify and understand the information more smoothly and provides a better overall reading experience.

If you need to repeat a sentence to emphasize it, you might need to vary its form, but otherwise, try to keep your structures the same for sentences with a similar function. For example: if you're giving solutions, then all of them should have a similar grammatical form so that the reader can automatically identify them.

Exercise

Revise the following sentences to produce consistent grammatical construction for the similar ideas expressed.

1. There is a considerable gap in the market for fashionable mountain wear among the Swiss, the Italians, the Spanish, and French.

....

2. Either you must query the invoice or provide payment.

....

3. Our client has ample experience in the South East Asian markets and in Japan.

....

4. It was both a long meeting and very tedious.

....

Answers

1. There is a considerable gap in the market for fashionable mountain wear among the Swiss, the Italians, the Spanish, and French.

   There is a considerable gap in the market for fashionable mountain wear among the Swiss, Italians, Spanish, and French.

2. Either you must query the invoice or provide payment.

   You must either query the invoice or provide payment.

3. Our client has ample experience in the South East Asian markets and in Japan.

   Our client has ample experience in the South East Asian and Japanese markets.

4. It was both a long meeting and very tedious.

   The meeting was both long and tedious.

Parentheses

If you add parentheses in the middle of a sentence to give extra information, use the same punctuation you would if the parentheses were absent.

Examples

I went to his office yesterday (my third attempt to see him), but he had left early.

She suggests (but with what evidence?) that a less aggressive pitch would be more effective with this client.

(If you need to add a full stop to the phrase in parentheses, the stop is placed inside the closing parenthesis.)

Quotations

Providing Evidence in Formal Reports and Emails

If you need to add direct quotations in formal writing, introduce them with a colon and then add the quotation marks.

Example

The provision of the contract is: "The first 5-year period has hard call protection."

*Vocabulary Note: **Hard Call Protection**

Hard call protection, or absolute call protection, is a provision included in callable bonds, which states that the bond issuer must wait until an agreed date before redeeming the bond.

Quotes that Do Not Provide Tangible Evidence Within a Sentence:

Seth Godin coined the phrase, "There's no shortage of remarkable ideas, what's missing is the will to execute them."

As Phil Knight said, "Play by the rules but be ferocious."

Begin a quotation of a full sentence or paragraph on a new line and center it, but there's no need for quotation marks if you don't want to use them.

Example

We can learn a lot from the words of President Obama:

The real test is not whether you avoid this failure because you won't. It's whether you let it harden or shame you into inaction, or whether you learn from it; whether you choose to persevere.

Quotations introduced by *that* are regarded as indirect and not placed within quotation marks.

Example

I can see from Branson's report that all the relevant safety measures have been adhered to.

Cliché expressions and famous phrases from popular culture do not need quotation marks.

Two heads are better than one.

Providing References

You may need to provide references in some formal reports, proposals, or presentations. If you're not sure how to do this, here is a quick reference guide to help you.

As a general practice, give references in parenthesis or in footnotes, not in the sentence's body. In-text references should include the surname of the author (or authors) and the date of publication.

Productivity is the maximization of available resources (Alexander & Raj, 2017)

If you are using a direct quote, include the page number as well.

"Productivity is the optimization of all available resources" (Alexander & Raj, 2017, p9)

If the author's name is included in the body of the text, add the date of publication in parentheses immediately afterward.

Alexander and Raj (2017) explain that management is the organization, motivation, and control of human activity directed to specific needs.

Full references should be included, in alphabetical order, at the end of the text. The punctuation of reference lists will differ slightly depending on the referencing style used but will generally follow the format:

Authors(s) Last name, First Initial. (Year published). *Title*. City: Publisher, Page(s)

For example:

Alexander, K. C, and Raj, Dr. A. K Ph.D. (2017) *Productivity Enhancement in Manufacturing Operations* Chennai: Notion Press, pp.9-11

Word Order

Where you choose to arrange words in a sentence communicates their relationship.

If feasible, keep words and groups of words connected in meaning and separate the ones that don't share a close connection.

There's a large reservoir in the area that we need to build around.

Should read:

We need to build around a large reservoir in the area.

Stick to the Word Order Rule

Although it often causes no issues in shorter, more straight forward sentences, you should stick to this rule because the interposed phrase or clause needlessly interrupts the natural order of the main clause. This can cause confusion and miscommunication when dealing with longer, more complex sentences.

In the first example above, when we read the sentence

"there's a large reservoir in the area that we need to build around,"

we cannot possibly know for certain whether the writer is saying that we need to build around the area or whether he or she is saying that we need to build around the reservoir.

The second version of this sentence leaves no room for interpretation:

"We need to build around a large reservoir in the area."

Exercise One

Rewrite the following sentence by reorganizing the words to make it clearer. You can check the suggested answer on the next page.

Wallace, in his latest report that he sent to us last month, gave a full justification for the recent overspend.

....

....

Answer

Wallace, in his latest report that he sent to us last month, gave a full justification for the recent overspend.

In his latest report last month, Wallace gave a full justification for the recent overspend.

⬇

The Relative Pronoun Goes After its Antecedent

As a rule, the relative pronoun should come immediately after its antecedent.

He wrote an article about his recent project, which was published in May's newsletter.

Should read:

He published an article in May's newsletter about his recent project.

This is the Chicago headquarters of Push Co., which is the subsidiary of S.P. Inc. It supplies the entire state of Illinois.

Should read:

This is the Chicago headquarters of Push Co., a subsidiary of S.P. Inc., which supplies the entire state of Illinois.

To avoid ambiguity, the following example should be rewritten.

A report to analyze the performance of our social media campaigns this year, which have produced varied results…

Instead, it should read:

A report to analyze the varied results of our social media campaigns this year…

Modifiers

Modifiers need to be, whenever feasible, with the word they are modifying.

All the members were not present.

Should read:

Not all the members were present.

He only found two mistakes.

Should read

He found only two mistakes.

Exercise Two

Rearrange the following sentence so that the modifiers are next to the word they are modifying.

Max Douglas will give a talk on Tuesday morning in Conference Room B, to which all staff members are invited, on the updated pay structure at 11 A.M.

Answer

Max Douglas will give a talk on Tuesday morning in Conference Room B, to which all staff members are invited, on the updated pay structure at 11 A.M.

On Tuesday morning at 11 A.M., Max Douglas will give in Conference room B a talk on the updated pay structure. All staff members are invited.

⬇

Some of these corrected examples may seem slightly unnatural to you, however they are a great way to avoid any miscommunications.

For example, the sentence:

On Tuesday morning at 11 A.M., Max Douglas will give in Conference room B a talk on the updated pay structure. All staff members are invited.

Can be expressed as:

On Tuesday morning at 11 A.M. in Conference room B, Max Douglas will give a talk on the updated pay structure. All staff members are invited.

This would not cause any confusion and is a very logical way of expressing the information. However, if you apply this structure in the following sentence:

On Tuesday morning at 11 A.M. in Rome, Max Douglas will give a virtual talk on the updated pay structure. All staff members are invited.

The problem with the above structure is that we now don't know whether the writer is telling us that the talk is at 11 A.M. local time in Rome or 11 A.M. wherever we are. There is an ambiguity which can lead to problems.

Therefore, the sentence should read:

On Tuesday morning at 11 A.M., Max Douglas will give in Rome a virtual talk on the updated pay structure. All staff members are invited.

OR

On Tuesday morning at 11 A.M., Max Douglas will give a virtual talk from Rome on the updated pay structure. All staff members are invited.

Split Infinitives

Avoiding split infinitives originally comes from Latin, where you cannot split an infinitive verb (to + verb) since it is considered one word for all intents and purposes.

Although English is largely Latin-based, it is arguably slightly more flexible than the Romance languages, so we often include an adverb between "to" and the verb to clarify what we mean in certain situations or add to the flow of a sentence.

There used to be a strict rule against using split infinitives, but nowadays, even the Oxford English Dictionary allows for the use of split infinitives to avoid "awkward, stilted sentences." (1)

(1) Guardian Newspaper, *"To boldly go for it: why the split infinitive is no longer a mistake,"* The Guardian Online, Sep 25th, 2017

Examples of split infinitives:

*to **really** see*

*to **actually** be*

*to **finally** launch a venture*

*to **overtly** support*

*to **gradually** decrease*

*to **more than** double*

How Can Splitting Infinitives Help My Communication? Sometimes, we need to split an infinitive to stop our sentences from being ambiguous or avoid sounding clumsy.

Exercise One

What is the difference in meaning between these three sentences?

Which one should you use?

A) *"The parties agreed to **quickly** dissolve the contract."*

B) *"The parties **quickly** agreed to dissolve the contract."*

C) *"The parties agreed to dissolve the contract **quickly**."*

Answers

Question 1

*A) "The parties agreed to **quickly** dissolve the contract."*

This sentence refers to the speed with which the contract was to be dissolved.

*B) "The parties **quickly** agreed to dissolve the contract."*

This sentence refers to the speed with which the parties were able to come to an agreement.

*C) "The parties agreed to dissolve the contract **quickly**."*

The sentence is slightly unclear. We can't be 100% sure whether the adverb "quickly" describes how the parties agreed or how the contract would be dissolved. It also looks slightly clumsy, and there's no emphasis on "quickly." It almost looks like it's been included as an afterthought.

Question 2

This is a trick question since it depends on the meaning you want to express. Options 1 and 2 are preferable.

⬇

Can I split Infinitives in Business Writing?

Generally speaking, it's best to avoid splitting infinitives in formal writing, as it is considered bad style, and splitting infinitives is not usually necessary when referring to factual matters.

There may be some instances where you can use a split infinitive when you are being general or vague.

For example,

We expect investment in this area to almost triple over the next decade.

Exercise Two

Unsplit these infinitives without changing the meaning of the sentence. You can reorder or rewrite the sentence if needed.

We expect the number of investors in this area to almost triple over the next five years.

XYZ Ltd. failed to properly allege damages.

Answers

We expect the number of investors in this area to increase/rise/grow by almost 300% over the next five years.

XYZ Ltd. failed to allege damages properly.

Subject-Verb Agreement

The subject of any sentence we write must coincide with the verb form we use. If the doer of the action in our sentence is plural, then the verb must be written in its plural form. The same applies the other way, so if the doer of the action is singular, then the verb form must also be singular.

For example:

"*The contract was canceled.*"

"*The accounts were forged.*"

Collective Nouns

Collective nouns are treated as singular entities in American English.

Example: "*The team is losing all its players to injury.*"

We can treat collective nouns as singular or plural in British English, though most British writers will gravitate towards the plural form.

Example: "*The **team are** losing all **their** players to injury.*"

Another example might be:

"*The **gift deeds were** submitted six days ago.*"

VS.

"*The **file with the gift deeds was** submitted six days ago.*"

This seems straightforward, but there can be issues when the collective noun is less clear.

Exercise One

Why is there a grammatical difference between *'a file'* and *'a number of'* or *'several'*? They are both collective nouns that refer to more than one individual within that collective. So, why the difference? Read the following two sentences and think about your answer. When you are ready, check your answer under the Answer section.

Sentence 1: *"The **file with the proposals was** submitted six days ago."*

VS.

Sentence 2: *"**Several proposals were** submitted six days ago."*

Answer:

In Sentence 1, the focal point of the message is 'the file.' We submitted the file, and there is only one file, so it's singular. However, in Sentence 2, the focus is on 'the proposals.' This is `plural.

This answer might be frustrating to some readers, as there are many nuances that can change the grammar of a sentence in English.

To go one step further and illustrate this, let's look at the following example:

"The **_number of new clients_** *we acquired last year* **_was_** *much higher."*

⬇

Exercise Two

Why is *'the number of'* suddenly singular in the above sentence?

We are still referring to more than one, so why is it now being treated as singular? Look at sentences 1 and 2 below and think about your answer. When you are ready, check the Answer section.

Sentence 1: "*A number of proposals were submitted six days ago.*"

Sentence 2: "*The number of new clients we acquired last year was much higher.*"

Answer:

The answer to this is the focus once more. Sentence 1, focuses on the plurality of the proposals. Meanwhile, Sentence 2 focuses on the change to 'the number.' Was the number higher or lower? It was higher. If we focus on the change to this number, we need to treat it as singular because it's a singular number.

⬇

It's also worth noting that some nouns can be treated as singular or plural depending on preference.

Example:

Charity

Private Limited Company

Public Limited Company

Option 1: *Alpha Beta Charlie* PLC <u>*are producers*</u> *of free-range animal products.*

VS.

Option 2: *Alpha Beta Charlie PLC <u>is a producer</u> of free-range animal products.*

Both the above options are 100% correct. However, since a company is considered a separate individual legal entity, the norm is to express these nouns in the singular when discussing official or legal matters.

When discussing non-official and non-legal matters, we can choose whether we write about the following nouns in singular or plural. The important thing is to remain consistent.

We must choose a practice and stick to it as much as possible, especially within the same document.

✔ Corporation
✔ Organisation
✔ Business
✔ Company

✔ Enterprise

✔ Prosecution

✔ Jury

Mixture of Singular and Plural Nouns

In the following example, several forms were sent to the NY office.

Therefore, we use the plural:

*"The non-disclosure agreement, the corporate bylaws, and the purchase agreement **were** all sent to our New York office on 23rd March."*

However, if we rewrite this sentence to focus the reader's attention on one particular document:

*"The non-disclosure agreement **was** sent to our New York office, **together with** corporate bylaws and the purchase agreement on 23rd March."*

The sentence's subject is now the *non-disclosure agreement,* so the verb needs to be singular.

When the subject of the sentence is an 'indefinite pronoun,' like the word *'each,'* we treat it as singular.

For example: *"**Each** of the forms **has** been filled out and sent to the relevant office."*

Sentences with Two Subjects

If the two subjects are singular, the verb stays singular:

"Neither the employment contract *nor the* loan agreement ***were*** *sent on time."*

Should be written as:

"Neither the employment contract *nor the* loan agreement ***was*** *sent on time."*

If one of the subjects is plural, we use a plural verb.

*"Neither the <u>employment contracts</u> nor the <u>loan agreement</u> **were** sent on time."*

*"Neither the <u>employment contract</u> nor the <u>loan agreements</u> **were** sent on time."*

Verbs VS Nouns

When we turn a base verb into a noun, this is called "nominalization." While it is very useful when we want to add variety to our professional writing, it can sometimes affect the power and meaning of our sentences.

Very noun-heavy sentences tend to be more watered-down in meaning since verbs carry more urgency and power.

They are also less direct and longer, sometimes making them convoluted.

Examples:

*The court **made the decision to grant** an injunction against Sean McFarlane after careful consideration.*

*The court **granted** an injunction against Sean McFarlane after careful consideration.*

The second sentence is better since it's clearer, more direct, and shorter.

Exercise

The following sentences are quite noun-heavy and would be better expressed more directly.

Transform them to make them clearer and more concise.

The considerable increase in crime over the past year has led to pressure being put on the police force (for a solution).

_____

The removal of the ambiguities in the contract made it look much clearer.

_____

Answers

Crime has increased considerably over the past year, and the police force is under pressure to find a solution.

The ambiguities in the contract were removed, which made it much clearer.

Ending with a Preposition

This traditional guideline also comes from a rule used in Latin, where it is grammatically incorrect and nonsensical to end any sentence with a preposition. In many Romance languages, putting a preposition at the end of a sentence can make it unintelligible in many cases.

In English, on the other hand, it depends on the audience. Some readers adhere to this guideline strictly and, in some cases, will judge your writing to be sloppy if you end a sentence with a preposition. Therefore, if we are writing for a more traditional audience, we might want to avoid ending our sentences with prepositions.

Examples:

Option 1: <u>Ending with a preposition</u>

Advantages: More relaxed, direct, and clearer sentences.

Disadvantage: Might be judged poorly by some more traditional readers.

Example: *She is one of the few secretaries he enjoys working with.*

Option 2: <u>Restructuring your sentence to avoid ending with a preposition</u>

Advantages: Much more formal. It will satisfy more traditional readers.

Disadvantage: It depends on the type of writing. It can be quite impersonal in some cases, like in semi-formal emails to colleagues or clients. It is not as direct and clear as ending with a preposition in most cases.

Example: *She is one of the few secretaries with whom he enjoys working.*

The Problem with Obsessing Over the Preposition Guideline

English isn't Latin and is not structured in the same way as Italian, Spanish, etc. Therefore, the rules that apply there aren't always fully transferable to English.

When we speak, we do not always know how we will end our sentences. There are idioms and phrasal verbs in English that require the speaker or the writer to end some sentences with prepositions. This is not imposed by artificial, arbitrary rules; it's a requirement of real-world communication. It's important to remember that this is exactly what a language is designed to do.

English is and should always be a constantly evolving tool for effective, purposeful communication. If we abandon this primary goal, we start to lose sight of what is important.

As Winston Churchill once said, *"Correcting my grammar is something up with which I will not put."*

"That" & "Which"

We use *"that"* to add a clause that defines exactly what we are talking or writing about. This clause should narrow the focus of the topic we are treating.

We use *"which"* to connect a clause that doesn't add extra focus on the discussion topic. This clause doesn't narrow down the topic.

Although *"that"* and *"which"* are often treated interchangeably in spoken English, when we are writing, our readers do not have the luxury of being able to infer meaning from our tone of voice and pauses. Therefore, it is vitally important that we pay attention to this rule.

The following two sentences illustrate the significance of using *"that"* and *"which"* correctly in writing:

Example 1: *The evidence* **that** *Mr. Miyagui presented to the judge was far from reliable.*

Meaning: This sentence means that of the larger body of evidence, the specific evidence presented by Mr. Miyagui wasn't reliable.

Example 2: *The evidence,* ***which*** *Mr. Miyagui presented to the judge, was far from accurate.*

Meaning: This sentence means that Mr. Miyagui presented all the evidence available, and it wasn't reliable.

As you can see, there is a huge difference in meaning.

Conjunctions

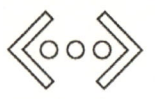

We can connect two ideas or concepts in a single sentence, as long as we use the right conjunction. Conjunctions are essentially words that connect.

Look at the following example, which is missing a conjunction:

"The notice was served on 21 July, no response has been received."

How can you fix this sentence? Rewrite it below:

Answer:

The sentence would be better if we wrote it as follows:

"The notice was served on 21 July, **but** *no response has been received."*

In the answer above, the two parts of the sentence are linked by the conjunction **'but.'**

We could also start the sentence with *'although'*:

Rewrite the sentence using the word *'although.'*

Answer:

*"**Although** the notice was delivered on 21 July, no response has been received."*

We can also express the same meaning using punctuation.

In the above example, we could use a **semicolon**:

Rewrite the sentence using a semicolon:

Answer:

"The notice was served on 21 July; no response has been received."

⬇

We can also use two sentences instead of one by using *'However'*:

Split the original sentence into two sentences using the word *'However.'*

Answer:

"The notice was served on 21 July. **However,** *no response has been received."*

Please Note: there should be a full stop or a semicolon in front of *'**however**'* if it introduces a new clause.

The Rule of the Last Antecedent

Words and groups of words that describe other words or groups of words are called 'modifiers.' We need to include any modifiers as closely as we can to the words they describe. Misplacing modifiers can lead to major misunderstandings and ambiguity.

According to the last antecedent rule, if you add a modifier at the end of a list, this modifier only applies to the last item mentioned on that list.

For example:

"Trucks, motorbikes, and cars in New York."

If we interpret this sentence literally, it refers to trucks and motorbikes from non-specific cities or regions. The only vehicles from New York we are referring to are the cars. This is extremely tricky because, in most written and spoken English, the communicator and the audience know that the trucks are from NY, the motorbikes from NY, and the cars from NY. It's implied in the sentence.

Pay attention to the rule of the last antecedent when producing any writing that is official, formal, or technical.

Exercise

What is the difference in meaning between these two sentences?

Option 1:

*Power issues **almost** led to 200 trains having to be canceled nationwide yesterday.*

Option 2:

*Power issues led to **almost** 200 trains having to be canceled nationwide yesterday.*

Answer:

Option 1:

Power issues almost led to 200 trains having to be canceled nationwide yesterday.

Meaning: The cancelations were narrowly avoided. The exact number of trains was 200.

Option 2:

Power issues led to almost 200 trains having to be canceled nationwide yesterday.

Meaning: The cancelations were not avoided, and almost 200 trains were canceled. It wasn't exactly 200 trains, the number was slightly lower, but we don't know exactly how many from the sentence.

Adding Descriptive Information with -ing phrases

We need to be careful not to complicate and distort our message when we add extra information using -ing verbs.

Exercise

Which sentence is clearer in meaning and easier to read? Why?

Option 1:

Sitting outside the meeting room, the client was updated on the current situation by the project manager.

Meaning: --

Option 2:

Sitting outside the meeting room, the project manager updated his client on the current situation.

Meaning: --

Answers:

Option 1:
Sitting outside the meeting room, the client was updated on the current situation by the project manager.

Meaning: Who was sitting outside the room? The client? The project manager? Both? We can't be 100% sure.

Option 2:
Sitting outside the meeting room, the project manager updated his client on the current situation.

Meaning: We know for certain that the project manager was outside the room in this sentence. The client may have been there physically too or may have been on the phone, but the sentence is clear and organized. It conveys as much meaning as possible with fewer words. Because it's immediately clearer, it makes it easier to read.

Thank you

I hope that you've found this business grammar, punctuation and style book useful. A lot of hard work has gone into this project.

The whole point of this book is to help you improve your writing in business and professional settings. Review any sections that you feel you need to and use them as a starting point for further research and practice.

You might have finished this book, but I hope that this is the start of a new journey for you.

Successful business writing is as much about reaching your personal goals as it is about helping others. It's give and take, happy mediums, win-win, all that and more.

Now you know how to:

- Structure your written messages and create a clear conversation.

- Come across as smarter, more confident, and more capable through plolished writing.

- Save time when it comes to writing, by maintaining clear objectives and organization.

- Prevent conflict and stress by making your points and intentions clear and honest, but at the same time diplomatic.

What Next?

In the next few pages, you'll find a massive bundle of free resources you can get hold of, including 300+ legal and business contracts and documents, and 100+ business letter and email templates! As a free member with exclusive access to my free starter library, you'll also get free reports, books and articles to help you take your career or business to the next level!

If you enjoyed this book, I'd be very grateful if you'd post a short review on Amazon. Your support really does make a difference and means a lot to me. I read all the reviews personally, so I can get your feedback and make this book even better in the future.

Thanks for your support.

Marc Roche

700+ Business Communication Resources FOR FREE

Sign up for the no-spam newsletter here www.macsonbell.com/free-toolbox-sign-up-form and get lots more exclusive content, all for FREE!. The resources include

300+ Legal and Business Document Templates (sign up FREE to receive the download link)

100+ Business Emails and Letter templates (sign up FREE to receive the download link)

DOWNLOAD your 300 PPT Templates here

https://drive.google.com/open?id=1oArc1iu3xJSgspmOK6PYRpVuk3F_Wqsh

+ Free Books

+ High Value Weekly Emails

Marc Roche. Macson Bell ® www.macsonbell.com

Free Bonus: 300+ Presentation Templates for PowerPoint

Here, you will find a downloadable database of 300+ Premium PowerPoint presentation templates, which you can use or edit as you please.

https://drive.google.com/open?id=1oArc1iu3xJSgspmOK6PYRpVuk3F_Wqsh

Sign up for our free resource newsletter, to receive more free resources! ☺

I hope you have found this book useful. Thank you for reading.

Get 300+ Legal and Business Document Templates

AND

100+ Business Emails and Letter templates

HERE:

www.macsonbell.com/free-toolbox-sign-up-form

About the Author

MARC ROCHE is a Business Writing & Professional Development Coach, writer, and entrepreneur.

He has worked with organizations such as the British Council, the Royal Melbourne Institute of Technology, and the University of Technology Sydney. Marc has also collaborated with Nike, GlaxoSmithKline, and Bolsas y Mercados.

Marc is originally from the UK and studied Business Management & Business Law at university before gaining his teaching qualification.

He likes to travel, cook, write, play sports, watch football, and spend time with friends and family in his free time.

Learn more about Marc at amazon.com/author/marcroche

Make sure to look at the free training resources for students and teachers at www.macsonbell.com/free-toolbox-sign-up-form

www.macsonbell.com

Macson Bell Coaching ®

Copyright © 2022 **Marc Roche**

Copyright © 2022 by Marc Roche & Macson Bell Business English ®. All Rights Reserved.

No part of this business writing, grammar, punctuation and style book may be reproduced, distributed, or transmitted in any form or by any means, including photocopying, recording, or other electronic or mechanical methods, or by any information storage and retrieval system without the prior written permission of the publisher, except in the case of very brief quotations embodied in critical reviews and certain other non-commercial uses permitted by copyright law.

2022 Macson Bell Business English©. All rights reserved

Made in the USA
Las Vegas, NV
27 July 2023